I0820836

PREHISTORIC LIFE

DINOSAURS RULE

—THE CRETACEOUS PERIOD—

by
Dougal Dixon

Ursa Books, an imprint of Bearport Publishing by FlutterBee

Credits

Cover, © Herschel Hoffmeyer/Shutterstock; 3, © Seamless Ahamad/Shutterstock; 4M, © Lee-Chu/Shutterstock; 4B, © Christian Jegou Publiphoto Diffusion/Science Source; 4–5, © Mohamad Haghani/Alamy Stock Photo; 5M, © Adwo/Shutterstock; 6M, © Stocktrek Images, Inc./Alamy Stock Photo; 6B, © The Natural History Museum, London/Science Source; 6–7, © Public Domain/Wikimedia Commons; 7B, © Public Domain/Wikimedia Commons; 8–9, © Mat Edwards; 8M, © Danny Ye/Shutterstock; 9T, © Michael Rosskothen/Shutterstock; 9B, © Warpaint/Shutterstock; 10–11, © Daniel Eskridge/Shutterstock; 10M, © Radiokafka/Shutterstock; 10B, © Daniel Eskridge/Shutterstock; 11T, © Elenarts/Shutterstock; 11M, © Michael Rosskothen/Shutterstock; 12–13, © Elenarts/Shutterstock; 12M, © YuRi Photolife/Shutterstock; 12B, © Igor Karasi/Shutterstock; 13B, © Warpaint/Shutterstock; 14–15, © warpaint/Shutterstock; 14M, © Timothy J. Bradley/Shutterstock; 14B, © Warpaint/Shutterstock; 15BL, 15BM, and 15BR, © YuRi Photolife/Shutterstock; 16–17, © Mat Edwards; 16M, © Catmando/Shutterstock; 16B, © Arcturus Image Bank; 17T, © Arcturus Image Bank; 18–19, © Daniel Eskridge/Shutterstock; 18M, © Herschel Hoffmeyer/Shutterstock; 18B, © Darya Lisavenka/Shutterstock; 19B, © Daniel Eskridge/Shutterstock; 20–21, © Mat Edwards; 20M, © Catmando/Shutterstock; 20B, © Arcturus Image Bank; 21T, © Arcturus Image Bank; 22–23, © YuRi Photolife/Shutterstock; 22T, © Dotted Yeti/Shutterstock; 22B, © SciePro/Shutterstock; 23T, © YuRi Photolife/Shutterstock; 24–25, © Mat Edwards; 24M, © Daniel Eskridge/Shutterstock; 24B, © Lefteris Papaulakis/Shutterstock; 25B, © kamomeen/Shutterstock; 26–27, © Herschel Hoffmeyer/Shutterstock; 26M, © Herschel Hoffmeyer/Shutterstock; 26B, © Warpaint/Shutterstock; 27T, © EreborMountain/Shutterstock; 28–29, © rodos studio/Shutterstock; 28T, © kamomeen/Shutterstock; 28B, © Catmando/Shutterstock; 29B, © kamomeen/Shutterstock; 30–31, © Mat Edwards; 30T, © Martin Weber/Shutterstock; 30BL, © Catmando/Shutterstock; 30BML, © kamomeen/Shutterstock; 30BM, © Catmando/Shutterstock; 30BMR, © kamomeen/Shutterstock; 30BR, © Catmando/Shutterstock; 31B, © kamomeen/Shutterstock; 32–33, © Daniel Eskridge/Shutterstock; 32T, © Ralf Juergen Kraft/Shutterstock; 32B, © kamomeen/Shutterstock; 33T, © Herschel Hoffmeyer/Shutterstock; 34–35, © Daniel Eskridge/Shutterstock; 34B, © Dotted Yeti/Shutterstock; 35T, © Kim Willems/Shutterstock; 35M, © Morphart Creation/Shutterstock; 35B, © SciePro/Shutterstock; 36–37, © Elenarts/Shutterstock; 36B, © Herschel Hoffmeyer/Shutterstock; 37M, © kamomeen/Shutterstock; 37B, © Herschel Hoffmeyer/Shutterstock; 38–39, © Catmando/Shutterstock; 38B, © Catmando/Shutterstock; 39M, © Catmando/Shutterstock; 39B, © Herschel Hoffmeyer/Shutterstock; 40–41, © Daniel Eskridge/Shutterstock; 40M, © Dotted Yeti/Shutterstock; 41T, © Catmando/Shutterstock; 41B, © Dotted Yeti/Shutterstock; 42–43, © Science Photo Library/Alamy Stock Photo; 42M, © Elena Elenaphotos21/Alamy Stock Photo; 42B, © Albert Wright/Alamy Stock Photo; 43B, © Nishath Riswan/Shutterstock; 44, © Arcturus Image Bank; 45T, © Michael Rosskothen/Shutterstock; 45B, © Mat Edwards; 47B, © Warpaint/Shutterstock.

Bearport Publishing Company Product Development Team

Kayla Eggert, Theresa Emminizer, Kim Jones, Allison Juda, Cole Nelson, Naomi Reich, Steve Scheluchin, Tiana Tran

Statement on Usage of Generative Artificial Intelligence

Bearport Publishing remains committed to publishing high-quality nonfiction books. Therefore, we restrict the use of generative AI to ensure accuracy of all text and visual components pertaining to a book's subject. See BearportPublishing.com for details.

Library of Congress Cataloging-in-Publication Data is available at www.loc.gov or upon request from the publisher.

ISBN: 979-8-89577-741-1 (hardcover)
ISBN: 979-8-89577-749-7 (ebook)

For more information, write to Bearport Publishing, 3500 American Blvd W, Suite 150, Bloomington, MN 55431. Printed in the United States of America.

Contents

The Rule of the Dinosaurs

Dinosaurs were the largest and most widespread creatures on land during the Cretaceous Period, which lasted from about 145 million years ago until about 66 million years ago. At the time, Earth was much warmer than it is today. This allowed plant life to thrive all over the planet, which created lots of food for large creatures, including the mighty dinosaurs.

Shifting Continents

The supercontinent of Pangaea formed during the late Carboniferous Period 300 million years ago. By the late Cretaceous Period, the continents we know today were starting to split apart. This process took millions of years, but it created a range of environments that allowed dinosaurs to adapt and diversify.

Large reptiles and bony fish lived in the inland seas of the Cretaceous Period.

The High Seas

Sea levels rose higher than ever during the Cretaceous Period, reaching as much as 800 feet (240 m) higher than current levels. Land covered only about 18 percent of Earth's surface. Some continents, such as North America, were divided by inland seas. This meant marine life became just as abundant as life on land.

Extra Large

The largest dinosaur of the Cretaceous was more than 1,000 ft. (300 m) long. How did this creature get so big? Scientists have suggested that intense competition between hunters may have encouraged all dinosaurs to grow. They also believe it is possible that these herbivores needed to reach higher to find food in tall trees.

Patagotitan was so large that its thigh bone alone was as tall as an adult human.

Plant Life of the Cretaceous

Many scientists believe that one of the reasons dinosaurs grew so large was that plants had grown and adapted so rapidly during the Cretaceous Period. During this time, flowering plants first appeared on Earth. Trees that we would recognize today, such as figs, willows, and magnolias, were also becoming widespread.

Flowers Spread

Scientists think flowering plants, or angiosperms, first evolved around the equator but quickly spread out from there. They were able to grow in environments where previous plants had struggled to survive. This adaptability made them so successful that they replaced the ferns and conifers that had previously dominated some regions.

Many early angiosperms thrived in places that had frequent wildfires.

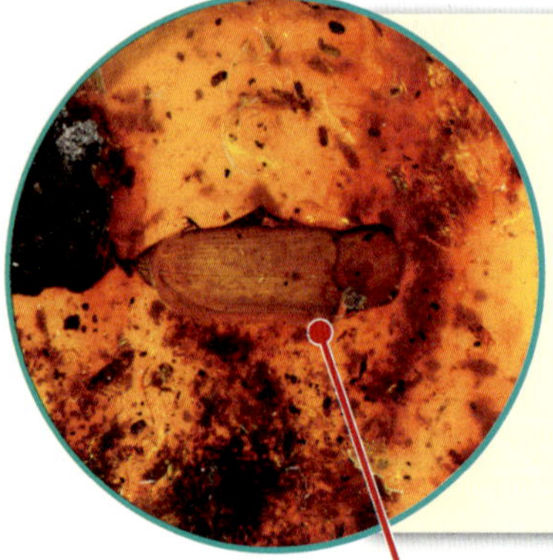

The relationship between beetles and angiosperms has lasted into the modern day. Many plants, such as magnolia trees, still rely on beetles to spread pollen.

Pollinators

Angiosperms need to share pollen between flowers to create seeds and grow new plants. At first, pollen was carried only on the wind. But soon, insects began to help spread pollen faster. Beetles were one of the first pollinating insects. They ate leaves and petals off flowering plants and picked up pollen as they did so.

CAMBRIAN	ORDOVICIAN	SILURIAN	DEVONIAN	CARBONIFEROUS	PERMIAN	TRIASSIC	JURASSIC	CRETACEOUS	CENOZOIC
								130 MYA (Million Years Ago)	

Name: *Monteschia vidalii* (mon-tee-SKI-ah *vi*-DAH-lee)

Order: Angiospermae

PLANT PROFILE

Montsechia vidalii are among the earliest known flowering plants that we have fossils of. The plant is sometimes called the first flower.

Scientists believe this plant grew underwater in shallow lakes around what is now central Spain.

Though it was one of the first flowering plants, *Monteschia vidalii* did not rely on animals for pollination. Instead, pollen would have floated through the water into the plant's flowers.

DID YOU KNOW? Scientists think that during the Cretaceous Period even the polar regions were warm enough to be partially covered in forests.

Diplodocus

The biggest of the plant eaters at the end of the Jurassic Period and the start of the Cretaceous were the long-necked sauropods. In fact, they were the biggest land animals ever. These dinosaurs developed into two major groups: the diplodocids, which were long and low; and the macronarians, which were tall, but not as long. The most famous of the diplodocids was *Diplodocus* itself.

Powerful tendons in its long neck allowed *Diplodocus* to hold its head very far from its body.

Dinosaur Celebrity

An almost complete fossil of *Diplodocus* was unearthed in 1899 by an expedition funded by Scottish-American steel tycoon Andrew Carnegie. Once the skeleton was assembled in his museum in Pittsburgh, Pennsylvania, Carnegie was so pleased with it that he had plaster casts made of all 292 bones. He sent copies of the skeleton to the museums of several capital cities throughout the world. As a result, in the early twentieth century, *Diplodocus* was the best known of all dinosaurs.

The skull of *Diplodocus* was as big as that of a horse. But its head was small compared with its body.

***Diplodocus*'s teeth were like the teeth of a comb. They could rake twigs and leaves from low-growing plants.**

DID YOU KNOW? A partial skeleton of a *Diplodocus* that may have been 110 ft. (33 m) long was found in 1991.

A Long Reach

Diplodocus's neck had at least 15 vertebrae and was 21 ft. (6.5 m) long. It reached out forward almost horizontally from the shoulders. This dino could swing its neck from side to side in a broad arc, reaching low-growing plants in front of it and at each side.

Because its body was balanced at the hips, *Diplodocus* could also reach up on its hind legs to feed from high branches.

The long, narrow tail of *Diplodocus* consisted of around 80 bones. It was used as a whip against predators.

CAMBRIAN
ORDOVICIAN
SILURIAN
DEVONIAN
CARBONIFEROUS
PERMIAN
TRIASSIC
JURASSIC
CRETACEOUS
CENOZOIC

153 MYA

Name: *Diplodocus* (dip-LOH-doh-kus)
Clade: Sauropoda
Length: Up to 85 ft. (26 m)
Weight: Up to 15 tons (13.5 t)

ANIMAL PROFILE

Brachiosaurus

The second sauropod group were the macronarians. While diplodocids had long bodies, macronarians were remarkably tall. Unusually for dinosaurs, their forelegs were longer than their hind legs, and their shoulders were very high. This allowed them to reach up into the highest trees to feed on leaves, needles, and twigs.

The skull of *Brachiosaurus* has a huge space in the nose area, giving the head a domed appearance. *Macronarian* means big-nosed.

The Towering Giant

Brachiosaurus was one of the first macronarians to be discovered. Because scientists of the time didn't have enough information when fossils of other macronarians were found, they originally thought all of these animals were the same. However, we now know that many of these discoveries were of creatures closely related to *Brachiosaurus*, but they were actually different enough to be other species. *Brachiosaurus* lived alongside *Diplodocus* and the other diplodocids in North America at the end of the Jurassic Period.

This huge macronarian in the Berlin museum was once thought to be a *Brachiosaurus*. It is now identified as a *Giraffatitan*.

CAMBRIAN	ORDOVICIAN	SILURIAN	DEVONIAN	CARBONIFEROUS	PERMIAN	TRIASSIC	JURASSIC	CRETACEOUS	CENOZOIC
							150 MYA		

Name: *Brachiosaurus* (*brak*-ee-oh-SORE-us)
Clade: Sauropoda
Length: Up to 72 ft. (22 m)
Weight: Up to 52 tn. (47 t)

ANIMAL PROFILE

A Long-Lived Family

The macronarians appeared in the middle of the Jurassic Period and survived until the age of dinosaurs ended with the end of the Cretaceous Period. During that time, they spread throughout the world and developed many strange shapes.

Europasaurus was a smaller macronarian. It was the size of a cow and lived on islands.

The tail of *Brachiosaurus* was quite short. It was used to balance the movement of the neck and head.

The legs were held straight like pillars to support the great weight of the animal.

DID YOU KNOW? Some scientists think the *Brachiosaurus* fossils we have are of specimens that were not fully grown. An adult *Brachiosaurus* may have been even bigger.

Camptosaurus

Besides sauropods, the other major group of plant-eating dinosaurs was ornithopods, or bird-footed dinosaurs. While sauropods supported their big bodies on all fours, most ornithopods could walk on their hind legs.

Like other ornithopods, *Camptosaurus* had a beak at the front of its mouth with cheeks at each side to hold plant material while it chewed.

A Fast Plant Eater

Camptosaurus was a common ornithopod from the late Jurassic Period. It usually walked on its hind legs and kept its hands free, so that it could gather food. Its food was any plant material it could reach. Judging from the wear on its tightly packed teeth, these plants were very tough. Since the ornithopod had strong hind legs, it could run away from the big meat eaters of the time.

Dryosaurus was a small, ostrich-sized ornithopod that lived alongside *Camptosaurus*.

Pigeon-Toed

The term *bird-footed* comes from the arrangement of the bones of the foot of these dinosaurs. In the 1800s, scientists thought the feet were like those of a bird. This distinguished them from the sauropods, which had toes similar to the toes of a lizard.

An ornithopod's footprint has three toes. *Camptosaurus* also had a fourth, rear claw.

DID YOU KNOW? *Camptosaurus* could probably run 15 miles per hour (24 kph).

Quetzalcoatlus

The dinosaurs were among the mightiest creatures on land in the Cretaceous Period. The skies were a different story. By this time, there were many types of birds flying across Earth. But pterosaurs, which had first appeared in the Triassic Period, still ruled the skies.

Flying Dragon

With a wingspan as wide as a small airplane, *Quetzalcoatlus* was one of the first of the gigantic pterosaurs to be discovered by paleontologists. It belonged to a pterosaur group called the azhdarchids, which were all huge. They probably hunted on the ground. When they stood on land, *Quetzalcoatlus* and the other azhdarchids, such as *Hatzegopteryx*, were as tall as a modern giraffe.

The arms of *Quetzalcoatlus* worked as wings in flight. They were also strong enough to support the animal while it was walking on the ground.

CAMBRIAN	ORDOVICIAN	SILURIAN	DEVONIAN	CARBONIFEROUS	PERMIAN	TRIASSIC	JURASSIC	CRETACEOUS	CENOZOIC
								66 MYA	

Name: *Quetzalcoatlus* (*kets*-ul-koh-AT-lus)
Order: Pterosauria
Wingspan: Up to 40 ft. (12 m)
Weight: Up to 550 lb. (250 kg)

ANIMAL PROFILE

DID YOU KNOW? *Quetzalcoatlus* would have spent more of its time on the ground than in the air.

Look at Me!

Each of the big pterosaurs had a differently shaped head and jaw, depending on the food it ate. Their patterned crests also differed by species, so that they could be recognized by others of their kind.

Pterodaustro filtered tiny pond animals with its comblike teeth.

Tapejara had a crest of skin stretched between bony struts.

Long-crested *Thalassodromeus* had the largest crest of the pterosaurs.

Jakapil

Thyreophoran dinosaurs are known for the protective plates along their bodies. Most small thyreophorans lived during Triassic and early Jurassic times. But some, such as *Jakapil*, survived into the Cretaceous Period.

A Tough Little Beast

Jakapil was covered all over in small bony plates that protected its head, back, and limbs. But unlike others of its kind, *Jakapil* lived in what is now Argentina. Its fossils were the first sign of thyreophorans living anywhere outside the Northern Hemisphere.

The fact that *Jakapil* had tiny forelimbs compared with its longer rear limbs shows us that it walked on two feet.

Other small thyreophorans, such as *Scutellosaurus*, lived about 100 million years earlier than *Jakapil*.

CAMBRIAN | ORDOVICIAN | SILURIAN | DEVONIAN | CARBONIFEROUS | PERMIAN | TRIASSIC | JURASSIC | CRETACEOUS | CENOZOIC

95 MYA

Name: *Jakapil* (JAK-a-pil)
Clade: Thyreophora
Length: Up to 5 ft. (1.5 m)
Weight: Up to 15.5 lb. (7 kg)

ANIMAL PROFILE

Keep Out!

Earlier thyreophorans had very small and simple shield-like plates along their bodies. These later evolved into much larger and more impressive plates arranged lengthwise down the body. The weight of these plates meant that the biggest of these animals needed to spread out on four feet. But the smallest, including *Jakapil*, were light enough to walk on two feet.

DID YOU KNOW? *Jakapil* lived in damp oasis areas within desert environments.

Ichthyovenator

The big, meat-eating theropod dinosaurs usually hunted and ate other big dinosaurs. However, in the Cretaceous Period, there was a group of very large theropods called spinosaurs. They lived beside rivers and fed on fish. We can tell because scientists have found fish remains in the stomach contents of some fossilized skeletons.

Big Sailbacks

Most of the spinosaurs that we know about had sails on their backs supported by a fence of bony struts sticking up from their backbones. These may have been used for signaling, to adjust their body temperature, or to aid in swimming. *Ichthyovenator* was different from the other spinosaurs in that its sail was divided. Part of it was on the back, and part was on the tail.

At 46 ft. (14 m) long, *Spinosaurus* was the biggest of the spinosaurs. It was also the longest of all the meat-eating theropods.

Amphibious Dinosaur

We think that *Ichthyovenator* and the other spinosaurs lived in or near the water because their fossilized bones have the same chemical composition that can be found in water-living crocodiles and turtles. Some of this dinosaur's bones were quite heavy, which would have helped control its buoyancy.

One of the most complete spinosaur skeletons ever found is of *Baryonyx*. But strangely, this creature did not appear to have had a sail. It is possible the sail broke off before it was fossilized.

Name: *Ichthyovenator* (*ik*-thee-oh-VEN-ah-tor)
Clade: Theropoda
Length: Up to 34 ft. (10 m)
Weight: Up to 2.6 tn. (2.4 t)

ANIMAL PROFILE

DID YOU KNOW? *Ichthyovenator* was one of the smallest of the spinosaurs.

Dakotaraptor

Some of the fiercest meat-eating theropod dinosaurs were dromaeosaurids—the running lizards. These were usually small and hunted swift-running prey through the undergrowth. But some, such as *Dakotaraptor*, became very large.

The big animals of the Cretaceous plains probably had nothing to fear from *Dakotaraptor*. It likely would have hunted smaller prey.

Flightless Wings

Fossilized arm bones of *Dakotaraptor* show that it had long feathers. These must have been used for finding a mate or controlling the animal's steering while running because with a body as big as a bear, *Dakotaraptor* was too heavy to fly. It would have needed speed for chasing down its food.

Chicken-sized *Mononykus* was another Cretaceous theropod. It had a single strong claw on each hand and probably ate ants and termites.

CAMBRIAN | ORDOVICIAN | SILURIAN | DEVONIAN | CARBONIFEROUS | PERMIAN | TRIASSIC | JURASSIC | CRETACEOUS | CENOZOIC

66 MYA

Name: *Dakotaraptor* (*da*-coh-ta-RAP-tuhr)
Order: Theropoda
Length: Up to 18 ft. (5.5 m)
Weight: Up to 770 lb. (350 kg)

ANIMAL PROFILE

A Loving Family of Killers

Dromaeosaurids, including *Dakotaraptor*, probably laid their eggs in nests, incubated them, and cared for their young after they hatched—very much like their bird descendants do. Scientists think this is true because we have found fossils of the nests and young of similar small dinosaurs.

DID YOU KNOW? *Dakotaraptor* was one of the last of the dromaeosaurids. It lived at the very end of the Cretaceous Period.

Deinocheirus

For 50 years, the fossil remains of a big dinosaur from Mongolia puzzled scientists. All they had were a pair of arms and hands with the most enormous fingers and claws they had ever seen. There were many guesses about who the owner of these limbs could be, but for years nobody had any idea just how odd this Cretaceous beast actually was.

A Strange Beast

When a pair of almost complete skeletons of this animal were eventually found, scientists realized that it was not just the hands that were strange. Despite being a theropod, it had the massive body and duck-like jaws of a herbivore. The huge claws were probably used for tearing down vegetation. Scientists determined that the creature belonged to a theropod group called the ornithomimids.

A typical ornithomimid, such as *Gallimimus*, was an elegant, fleet-footed, ostrich-sized theropod.

Therizinosaurus, with its small head and enormous claws, was a typical therizinosaur.

More Big Hands

Another dinosaur group with big hands were the therizinosaurs. These were also theropods, but while most other theropods ate meat, therizinosaurs actually ate plants. They may have used their long fingers with enormous scythe-like claws to pull down branches and rip off the leaves for food. These claws may have also been used for display, to frighten off enemies, or to attract mates.

DID YOU KNOW? Although this creature's arms were discovered in 1965, the rest of the skeleton of a *Deinocheirus* was not found until 2014.

Tyrannosaurus

The tyrannosaurids were one of the last meat-eating theropod groups to evolve. Although they started as small animals in the Jurassic Period, they later developed into the largest land-living meat eaters that ever lived. They dominated the continents of Asia and North America at the end of the Cretaceous Period.

Terrifying Hunter

The last of the meat-eating dinosaurs is probably the best known. The *Tyrannosaurus* had huge jaws in a heavy skull. It could focus its eyes on prey in front of it—a useful skill for hunting. Its ears were attuned to the sounds of animals walking on the ground, and it would likely hide and wait for that sound before ambushing its prey.

Majungasaurus, a member of a southern hemisphere group of abelisaurids, was the biggest meat eater in Cretaceous Africa.

The young *Tyrannosaurus* was almost like a different animal compared with its parent. It was long-jawed and swift-footed. It also hunted different prey.

Megaraptor was the biggest meat eater in South America during the late Cretaceous Period.

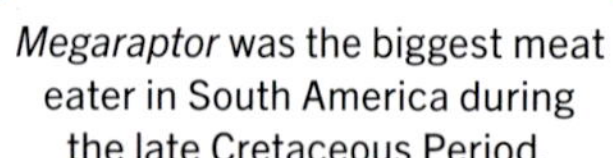

The Biggest Meat Eaters

It was not just *Tyrannosaurus* and its relatives that grew larger at the end of the Cretaceous Period. The theropod families on other continents developed huge forms as well, some of them almost reaching the size of *Tyrannosaurus*.

Name: *Tyrannosaurus* (ty-*ran*-oh-SORE-us)
Clade: Theropoda
Length: Up to 40 ft. (12.2 m)
Weight: Up to 7.7 tn. (7 t)

ANIMAL PROFILE

Alamosaurus

Nature saved the biggest dinosaurs for last! The sauropod group called the titanosaurs lived at the very end of the Cretaceous Period and included the biggest animals ever to live on land. They were part of the macronarian line, which included *Brachiosaurus*.

Each neck bone of *Alamosaurus* consisted of struts and flat plates arranged to make a lightweight structure with great strength.

Mountains of Flesh and Bone

The biggest of the titanosaurs have been found in South America, but *Alamosaurus* was the largest species in North America. It probably migrated from the south when a land bridge emerged between the two continents. There had been no sauropods in North America for the previous 30 million years, since the early Cretaceous Period.

Many species of titanosaur, such as *Saltasaurus*, had protective bony plates on the skin of their backs.

CAMBRIAN | ORDOVICIAN | SILURIAN | DEVONIAN | CARBONIFEROUS | PERMIAN | TRIASSIC | JURASSIC | CRETACEOUS (68 MYA) | CENOZOIC

Name: *Alamosaurus* (al-*ah*-moe-SORE-us)
Clade: Sauropoda
Length: Up to 100 ft. (30 m)
Weight: Up to 88 tn. (80 t)

ANIMAL PROFILE

Why So Big?

Many animals, such as theropods and crocodiles, grew very large at the end of the Cretaceous Period. But none grew as enormous as the titanosaurs. The sheer size of these creatures is difficult to imagine. *Patagotitan* was about as tall as a 10-story building! That's more than five times the height of a modern-day giraffe.

Fossilized stomach contents of *Alamosaurus* show that it ate all kinds of plants.

Titanosaurs had no toes. Their foot bones had turned into vertical columns to support their great weight.

DID YOU KNOW? Titanosaur remains have been found on all seven continents, including Antarctica.

Iguanodon

There were plenty of ornithopods in the Jurassic Period, but it was during the Cretaceous that they really came into their own. Toward the end of the period, they developed into a group called the duckbills. These creatures were the most varied and abundant plant eaters of their time.

Plant-Eating Reptile

One of the most famous of the ornithopods, and one of the first dinosaurs to be discovered, was from the earliest part of the Cretaceous Period. Its first fossils ever found were of teeth that scientists thought seemed to come from a big plant-eating reptile. They were like those of the modern plant-eating iguana. So, the animal was given the name *Iguanodon*, meaning iguana tooth.

Iguanodon walked on all fours, but it could raise itself on its big hind legs to feed from trees. Its hands could be used for both walking and grasping.

Many duckbills, such as *Olorotitan*, developed big, strangely shaped crests on the tops of their heads.

The Duckbills

A group of ornithopods called the duckbills developed from animals such as *Iguanodon*. They take their name from the beak at the front of their mouths, which became broad and flat similar to a duck's beak. The many types of duckbills had spread all across the world by the end of the Cretaceous Period.

Name: *Iguanodon* (ig-WAH-noh-don)
Clade: Ornithopoda
Length: Up to 35 ft. (11 m)
Weight: 5 tn. (4.5 t)

DID YOU KNOW? In 1878, about 40 skeletons of *Iguanodon* were found together in a coal mine in Belgium.

Triceratops

Ceratopsians were horned dinosaurs. Like most dinosaur groups, they started as small, rabbit-sized animals when they first appeared. But by the end of the Cretaceous Period, they were truly huge creatures with massive shields around their necks and horns on their faces.

Triceratops used its horns to defend against attacks from big meat eaters, such as *Tyrannosaurus*.

The Biggest Ceratopsian

The last of the ceratopsians was three-horned *Triceratops*. It looked a little like a rhinoceros, but with a frill around its neck. It had two long, forward-pointing horns above the eyes and a smaller horn on the snout. It lived in huge herds on the plains of what is now North America.

Other Ceratopsians

Toward the end of the Cretaceous Period, many types of ceratopsians appeared. While they had similar bodies, each had a different arrangement of horns and frills on the head.

Centrosaurus

Einiosaurus

Styracosaurus

Nasutoceratops

Diabloceratops

DID YOU KNOW? When the first *Triceratops* horns were discovered, they were thought to have come from a giant bison.

Ankylosaurus

With so many huge carnivorous dinosaurs around at the end of the Cretaceous Period, many of the plant eaters developed coverings of shields, plates, and scales to protect themselves. These worked like protective chain mail. The thyreophorans, relatives of the Jurassic Period's *Stegosaurus*, became the most heavily defended of all.

A Living Tank

Ankylosaurus was the most heavily protected of all the thyreophorans. Its head and back were covered with strong bony knobs, and it had a massive club at the end of its tail. Even its eyelids were like steel shutters. The biggest meat eaters of the time would have found it difficult to bite through these barriers.

Some scientists used to think that the club of *Ankylosaurus* had eye spots to confuse predators, but many now doubt this.

The end of the tail was made of solid bone, and the bones in the tail were fused together so that it could be swung around like a club.

CAMBRIAN | ORDOVICIAN | SILURIAN | DEVONIAN | CARBONIFEROUS | PERMIAN | TRIASSIC | JURASSIC | CRETACEOUS | CENOZOIC

66 MYA

Name: *Ankylosaurus* (an-*kye*-low-SORE-us)
Clade: Thyreophora
Length: Up to 33 ft. (10 m)
Weight: Up to 8.8 tn. (8 t)

ANIMAL PROFILE

Club or Spike?

There were two main types of thyreophorans at the end of the Cretaceous. One type was the ankylosaurs, which had clubs at the ends of their tails. The other was the nodosaurs, which had no tail clubs but defended themselves with huge spikes on their shoulders.

DID YOU KNOW? We have never found a complete skeleton of *Ankylosaurus*, but scientists can guess what it looked like by studying its more complete relatives.

Mosasaurus

The really big hunters in the oceans at the very end of the Cretaceous Period were mosasaurs. They belonged to the squamate group—the same group that contains today's lizards and snakes. Their closest living relatives are monitor lizards, such as the komodo dragon.

The jaws of *Mosasaurus* were long and narrow, perfect for moving smoothly through the water and for catching fish.

Sea Lizard

Mosasaurus was a bit like a giant monitor lizard but with legs and feet shaped like paddles and a fluke at the ends of its tail. With its tail, paddles, and streamlined shape, it had the same adaptations for a swimming lifestyle as earlier ichthyosaurs.

Mosasaurus and most other mosasaurs had sharp teeth for catching fish. However, a few had rounded teeth for cracking shellfish.

The toes of *Mosasaurus* were fused together to form a swimming paddle.

A New Idea

When the jawbones of *Mosasaurus* were excavated from a Dutch quarry in 1764, they helped confirm to scientists that extinction could happen. The idea that whole groups of animals could become extinct was completely new.

The first *Mosasaurus* fossils found were of their huge, lizard-like jaws.

We know of about 40 different types of mosasaurs.

Name: *Mosasaurus* (*moe*-zah-SORE-us)
Order: Squamata
Length: Up to 56 ft. (17 m)
Weight: Up to 86 tn. (78 t)

ANIMAL PROFILE

DID YOU KNOW? Mosasaurs competed with the ichthyosaurs for food.

Deinosuchus

It is often said that crocodiles have remained unchanged since the days of the dinosaurs. This is broadly true, and there were some prehistoric crocodiles that looked very much like today's cold-blooded hunters. But modern crocodiles are much smaller. In the Cretaceous Period, some of them were huge!

Terror of the Swamp

Deinosuchus was a giant crocodile that lived in what is now North America. It preferred brackish water and lived in coastal swamps and river mouths, where it hunted its prey. Bite marks on fossilized bones show that it likely hunted large dinosaurs—even ones as big as the tyrannosaurs!

Sarcosuchus, a relative of *Deinosuchus*, was the terror of the African dinosaurs on the other side of the Atlantic Ocean.

The broad snout of *Deinosuchus* helped it seize unsuspecting prey and pull it into the water.

Like a modern crocodile, *Deinosuchus* lurked just below the water before leaping out at its prey.

Crocodilian Varieties

Other crocodiles from the Cretaceous Period included running crocodiles, fish-eating crocodiles, and even vegetarian crocodiles. However, only water-dwelling crocodiles that hunt by ambushing prey have survived into the modern day.

Kaprosuchus was a land-living hunting crocodile. Because of its huge tusks, it has been nicknamed the boar croc.

CAMBRIAN | ORDOVICIAN | SILURIAN | DEVONIAN | CARBONIFEROUS | PERMIAN | TRIASSIC | JURASSIC | CRETACEOUS (75 MYA) | CENOZOIC

Name: *Deinosuchus* (dy-no-SOO-kus)
Order: Crocodylia
Length: Up to 35 ft. (11 m)
Weight: Up to 5 tn. (4.5 t)

ANIMAL PROFILE

DID YOU KNOW? *Deinosuchus* continued to grow for most of its 50-year lifespan.

Dolichorhynchops

Back in the Jurassic Period, swimming plesiosaurs were divided into two groups: long-necked plesiosauroids and big-headed pliosauroids. By the end of the Cretaceous, plesiosauroids were still flourishing, but the pliosauroids were all gone. A new group of plesiosauroids developed to fill their place in the ecosystem.

A New Shape

Dolichorhynchops was the new long-headed plesiosaur of the Cretaceous Period. It combined the long jaws of the pliosauroids with the flexible neck of the earlier plesiosauroids. Like a modern whale, it needed to come to the surface regularly to breathe.

Dolichorhynchops was hunted by mosasaurs. Bones of one specimen have been found in the skeleton of the mosasaur *Tylosaurus*.

***Dolichorhynchops* did not need to come ashore to lay eggs. It gave birth to live young.**

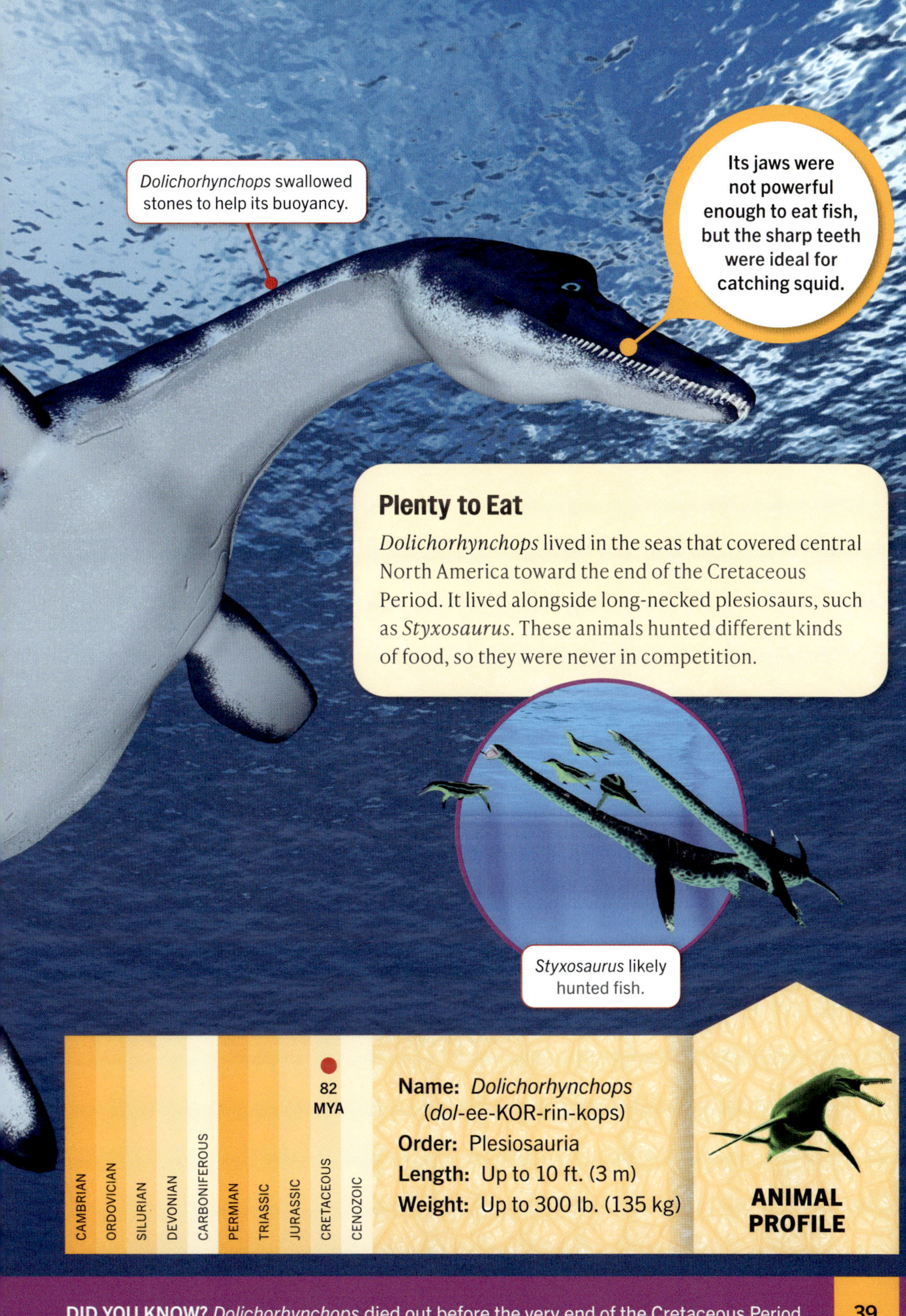

Plenty to Eat

Dolichorhynchops lived in the seas that covered central North America toward the end of the Cretaceous Period. It lived alongside long-necked plesiosaurs, such as *Styxosaurus*. These animals hunted different kinds of food, so they were never in competition.

Name: *Dolichorhynchops* (*dol*-ee-KOR-rin-kops)
Order: Plesiosauria
Length: Up to 10 ft. (3 m)
Weight: Up to 300 lb. (135 kg)

DID YOU KNOW? *Dolichorhynchops* died out before the very end of the Cretaceous Period.

Alphadon

Mammals appeared in the late Triassic Period, around the same time as the dinosaurs. While they did not grow to the same size, mammals did diversify greatly up to the extinction event at the end of the Cretaceous Period.

Delicate Fossils

Early mammals were so small that we don't often find fossils of them. We know about most of them only from fossils of teeth. These teeth were much harder than bones and could fossilize more easily. We can compare the fossil teeth with the teeth of modern mammals to figure out what kind of animal the fossils belonged to. From its teeth, we can tell that *Alphadon* was similar to modern opossums.

Alphadon and other mammals of the Cretaceous hid themselves in undergrowth, burrows, and trees, as well as beneath the foliage of flowering plants.

In the second half of the Cretaceous Period, there were many new forms of mammals appearing. This increase in diversity was probably caused in part by the different plants appearing at the time, which offered new types of food.

Dinosaurs certainly ruled the world at the end of the Cretaceous Period, but they were soon to be replaced by mammals.

Many Types

Mammals flourished in the undergrowth at the feet of the dinosaurs. In the Cretaceous Period, they developed many of the shapes and lifestyles that we still associate with small mammals. However, having the same shapes does not mean that they were closely related to today's small mammals. Almost all Cretaceous mammals belonged to groups that have since become extinct. Only a few survived to give rise to the mammals of today.

Purgatorius belonged to a group that survived the extinction event at the end of the Cretaceous Period. It may have been the ancestor of primates, including human beings.

Meat eating dinosaurs, such as *Stenonychosaurus*, hunted *Alphadon* and other small mammals.

Name: *Alphadon* (AL-fa-don)
Class: Mammalia
Length: Up to 1 ft. (30 cm)

DID YOU KNOW? *Alphadon* may have been a marsupial, meaning that it would have carried its young in a pouch on its body.

The End of the Dinosaurs

The Cretaceous Period was a time of amazing biodiversity, but it ended with the extinction of around 75 percent of life on Earth, including most of the dinosaurs. But though this catastrophe ended the age of dinosaurs, it set the stage for other animals to adapt and take over.

Mass Extinction

About 66 million years ago, an asteroid several miles wide hit Earth near the Yucatán Peninsula in what is now Mexico. The impact released enough dust into the air to block out sunlight for months or even years. This made temperatures much colder and meant plants could no longer photosynthesize. Without plants to feed on, large herbivores died off, and the carnivores that ate these animals soon followed.

The aftermath of the asteroid's impact threatened almost all life on Earth.

Lucky Mammals

Smaller burrowing animals, such as rodents, had the best chance of surviving the cold climate caused by the asteroid's impact. Animals that could survive on many different foods also had an easier time than those with more limited diets. Ultimately, this meant that many small, omnivorous mammals survived the extinction event at the end of the Cretaceous Period.

Mammals today are all descended from mouse-sized creatures.

Modern Dinosaurs

Not all of the dinosaurs went extinct at the end of the Cretaceous Period. Birds are descended from two-legged theropods. Some Cretaceous theropods had feathers as well as the ability to stand upright on two legs. But just like birds today, not all theropods with feathers could fly.

Birds like the helmeted hornbill have a strong resemblance to their dinosaur ancestors.

Review and Reflect

Now that you've read about life in the Cretaceous Period, let's review what you've learned. Use the following questions to reflect on your newfound knowledge and integrate it with what you already knew.

Check for Understanding

1. How did early beetles help flowering plants spread during the Cretaceous Period? *(See p. 6)*
2. What feature of *Diplodocus*'s neck helped it feed without moving its body much? *(See p. 8)*
3. How did the front legs of *Brachiosaurus* help it feed from the tallest trees? *(See p. 10)*
4. What purpose did the crests of *Quetzalcoatlus* likely serve? *(See p. 15)*
5. Why was the discovery of *Jakapil* fossils in Argentina important? *(See p. 16)*
6. What evidence suggests *Ichthyovenator* lived in or near water? *(See p. 18)*
7. What do scientists think *Dakotaraptor* used its feathers for? *(See p. 20)*
8. What adaptations made *Tyrannosaurus* such an effective ambush hunter? *(See pp. 24–25)*
9. How many continents have titanosaur fossils been discovered on? *(See p. 27)*
10. What information do the teeth of an *Iguanodon* reveal about its diet? *(See p. 28)*
11. What physical features helped *Triceratops* defend itself from predators? *(See pp. 30–31)*
12. Describe two features of *Ankylosaurus* that protected it. *(See pp. 32–33)*
13. Why was the discovery of *Mosasaurus* fossils significant? *(See p. 35)*
14. What did *Dolichorhynchops* do to help control its buoyancy? *(See p. 39)*
15. How do paleontologists learn about the early mammals of the Cretaceous Period? *(See p. 40)*

Making Connections

1. Choose one of the giant sauropods (such as *Diplodocus*, *Brachiosaurus*, or *Alamosaurus*) and compare it with a modern-day large animal. How are they similar, and how are they different?

2. Explain the significance of fossilized teeth and what they can tell us about prehistoric animals.

3. Compare the hunting styles of *Tyrannosaurus* and *Dakotaraptor*. How did their physical features make them suited to hunt different kinds of prey?

4. Both *Ankylosaurus* and *Triceratops* had strong defenses against predators. How were their protective features different, and what might this tell us about each creature's behavior or the predators they faced?

5. *Alphadon* was a small mammal that lived alongside dinosaurs. How did it survive when the giant reptiles of the same time did not?

In Your Own Words

1. Which prehistoric creature in this book would you most like to see alive today? Where would you expect to find them in the modern world?

2. Imagine you found fossilized dinosaur teeth. What could these teeth tell you about the dinosaur's diet?

3. Do you think an animal like *Ankylosaurus*, with its heavy armor and tail club, would survive against today's predators? Why or why not?

4. Imagine dinosaurs never went extinct. How might Earth's ecosystems look different if these creatures still lived on Earth?

5. If you lived during the time of the dinosaurs, which animal do you think would be the most dangerous?

Glossary

amphibious living partly on water and partly on land

Cambrian a geological period lasting from 541 to 485 million years ago

Carboniferous a geological period lasting from 359 to 299 million years ago, in which there were many swamps and forests on Earth

clade a biological grouping of organisms that have a common ancestor

class a biological grouping smaller than a clade but larger than an order

crest a growth of bones, scales, feathers, skin, or hair on the head or back of an animal

Cretaceous a geological period lasting from 145 to 66 million years ago

Devonian a geological period lasting from 410 to 355 million years ago

evolution the process by which a species changes and adapts over time

extinction when an animal species has died out completely

family a biological group smaller than a class but larger than a genus

foliage the leaves of a plant

fossil prehistoric remains that have become preserved in rock

Jurassic a geological period lasting from 201 to 145 million years ago

keratin the material that makes up hair, feathers, hoofs, claws, and horns

mammal an animal that gives birth to live young and feeds them milk

order a biological grouping that is smaller than a class but larger than a family

predator an animal that hunts and eats other animals

prey an animal that is hunted and eaten by other animals

primates an order of mammals that includes humans, monkeys, apes, and lemurs

reptile a scaly animal that is cold-blooded and usually lays eggs

species a biological group that is smaller than a genus and includes organisms that can produce offspring together

Triassic a geological period lasting from 252 to 201 million years ago

Read More

Batty, Tim. *Tiny Dinosaurs (Dinosaur Discovery).* New York: Rosen Publishing Group, 2023.

Gifford, Clive. *Dinosaurs (Super Tech).* Buffalo, NY: Enslow Publishers, 2026.

Martin, Claudia. *Exploring Fossils (Rocks & Fossils).* Minneapolis: Bearport Publishing, 2026.

Potter, William. *Dinosaurs and Other Prehistoric Life (Our World in Numbers).* New York: DK, 2024.

Learn More Online

1. Go to **FactSurfer.com** or scan the QR code below.
2. Enter "**Dinosaurs Rule**" into the search box.
3. Click on the cover of this book to see a list of websites.

Index